The

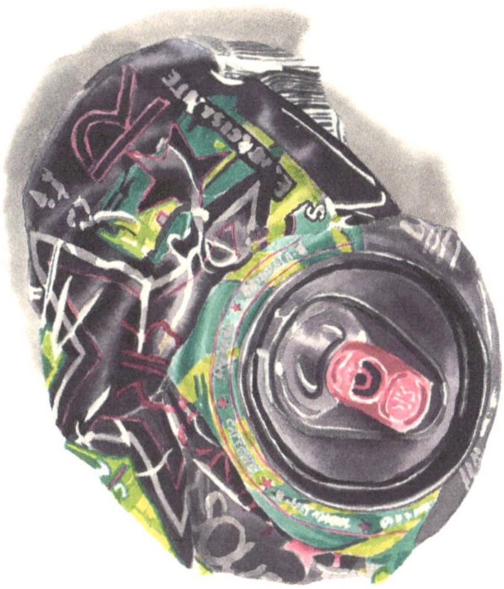

Poems

The

ANNA SWANSON

Garbage

ILLUSTRATIONS BY APRIL WHITE

Poems

BRICK BOOKS

Contents

The Garbage Poems

I Am Writing a Spell for Your Nervous System

and hiding it in a poem.
I know you're trying to stitch

the world back together
while it breaks and keeps

breathing. Like you. Another
heatwave, hurricane. Grief

gurgles like a sump pump.
The Arctic on fire. Thirsty birds

of industry, mouthing
dry wells. Bulldozers

in the olive grove. Prehensile
suits in a sealed building,

deciding who deserves
to be a person. Baby monitors

tuned to the evening news.
Deep time is breathing

hard. Your nerves: clenched
shut like barnacles and still

flinching. I am casting a road
out of the city. Stop waiting

for CNN to self-soothe.
Stop memorizing formulas

for herbal abortion, just
in case, even though

some futures are no longer
unimaginable. Here

is a highway that vanishes
behind you like wet footprints.

Gravel pullout, the rule
of three boulders across

an unmarked road. The car door
closing with a reverse bang,

retracting into itself
the invention of cars.

Because you are in a poem,
rusted mile markers appear

only for as long as you walk
the dirt road towards them.

Now a marshy spot, now
lily pads, now wooden pallets

thrown down for you to cross.
Labrador tea and pitcher plants

flanking a narrow trail that is
all you recall of the world.

An opening in the trees.
Worn stones sloping down

to the flickering mirror of a pond.
You step out of the idea of clothes,

into a shallow dive.
Fingertip-to-fingertip

with your reflection—
and gone. A beat later, slick

and blinking, as if from a dark
room: somersault, scissor kick,

glide. Your body diamond-tipped,
a stylus polishing a groove.

Practice this skin. A dark map
back here, sparking, neural.

When it is time, walk up out
of the pond, dripping with

what made you. The world
leans down over cupped palms

to blow you dry. When you are
ready for clothes to exist,

clothes. The path winks
into existence before you.

Eventually you think,
I had a car. Onward,

the scrappy pulse
of the world. And whatever

work you have to do,
you begin again.

SOME DEFINITIONS

beginning, *n.* Did it begin the first time I planned a week-long trip on the water and my body couldn't carry me there? Did it begin with the water? Did it begin with the distance between me and the water?

garbage, *n.* "Waste material, refuse, litter; filth; trash, rubbish, *esp.* food or household waste."—OED

garbage, *n.* I arrive at the retreat during a heatwave. The first morning, I walk out to the pools under the waterfall for a morning swim before the heat of the day brings the crowds. I am alone, naked with the water and the sky and the discarded evidence of yesterday's revels—beer cans, chip bags, a pop tart box, a sodden sock. The joy is stronger than the annoyance, but still. I haul out grocery bags of garbage the next morning, and the morning after.

failing, *v* I am staying in a small blue house on a cliff near the Atlantic Ocean to write about an illness that began twenty years ago at the edge of another ocean. I am sitting at the wooden table with the wide ocean view and failing, daily, to write the project that has funded this retreat. Will my concussed brain let me do this? I don't know. It's been five years. *I will be happy if I write anything,* I tell my brain. *I will take you swimming every day.* If this time were not funded, I would not be failing at sitting by the ocean. If this time were not funded, I would not be here. *Pick anything,* I tell my brain. *Please.*

litter, *n.* "Odds and ends, fragments and leavings lying about, rubbish; a state of confusion or untidiness; a disorderly accumulation of things lying about."—OED

found text, *n*. I spend a morning working on an erasure poem using British Petroleum's press release for their 2010 oil spill in the Gulf of Mexico, trying to force slippery corporate words—*elsewhere, injury, tremendous, hydrocarbons, shareholders, regret*—to say the violently unsaid. As I stand up to sort the morning's haul of bottles and cans and cartons from the river into garbage and recycling bins, I start reading the labels.

practice, *n*. I swim early, bringing home assorted garbage. I sort it on the kitchen table, copy out brand names, slogans, instructions, special offers, promises, ingredient lists, health warnings. Ants crawl out of sticky pop cans. The kitchen smells like stale beer. I use reading glasses to make out the fine print and clean my keyboard constantly. I sort, type, alphabetize, my skin still singing from the cold water.

constraint, *n*. I rearrange the words to create small proto-poems about the swimming hole. I can re-use words and combine them, but never shorten or split. If a word is torn, or partly worn off, I transcribe whatever fragment remains. I move the words around, flip them over in my brain like memory tiles trying to find something that feels like my voice within the peculiar diction of beer cans, fast food, and candy wrappers. For the titles, I give myself free reign. Every other word of a poem must be found or made by combining.

scaffold, *v*. Constraint provides a structure within which I can work on rebuilding my voice after the concussion. Not only does it resonate metaphorically—piecing together a voice out of fragments—it also helps strengthen and rebuild my injured brain's ability to write poetry. I am trying to say how hard it is to be in a body, or how joyous, I can't tell which.

failing, ***v.*** The rules make a space where I can fail at fluency by choice. How luxurious to hit a wall that isn't my own brain.

lexicon, ***n.*** The garbage words are shiny, pushy, sure of themselves. The swagger, the hyperbole, all the imperatives and superlatives. Language that marketing has soured, made meaningless, and that I will try to steal back from capitalism.

litter, ***n.*** A word we've been taught to use when we see consumer waste scattered across a landscape. A word that keeps us focused on whoever last touched these pop cans, beer bottles, and chip bags. That steers us away from questions about why disposable packaging exists and what else is possible. A word designed to protect corporate profit margins.

gesture goods, ***n.*** "Many disposable items like plastic bags or polystyrene clam shells or tissues can be considered as 'gesture goods.' They facilitate certain practices such as eating on the move or blowing your nose, and then leave as soon as that action is performed."—Gay Hawkins, "Disposability"

swimming, ***n.*** In the water, I can think clearly, focus, sustain an open and easily delighted attention. My body can't always get me to the water, but it can usually carry the feeling of the water back with me.

mikveh, ***n.*** A Jewish ritual cleansing involving immersion in living waters—ocean, river, rainwater collected in an in-ground pool—to mark or witness a life change or transformation.

Flatrock

All words (except titles) from garbage collected at a swimming hole in Flatrock, NL.

Throttle
ENERGY DRINK

For the Boys Cliff-Jumping by the Memorial Stone

We, the full throttle.
The cluster-pak of body, water, will.

We, the cold open falls, the certified fountains
of no moderation. We are this sunlight. This skin! Why?

Why not? We are the famous flavour.
We are the wonderful.

We adidas-punch our way into the water.
Twist-happy & thick with chances.

We are not sorry. We are
the ice that will not melt,

the special extract in the root beer of not aging,
the sparkling under-king, the carbonated wet dream,

the premium formula good stuff. We are,
at a price you do not know,

at any price,
this.

For the Two Girls in the Lower Pool, Kissing

Nothing quite like it:
your body wonderful, the water,

the biodegradable hand
on your skin, your skin

& the storm brewing below it.
Take this in, all particles of it.

There was risk, yes, & you swallowed it,
sparkling, to be where you are.

You know the cost of caution
is always more. That these warning fumes

are only unattended marketing.
Should not be inhaled.

May cause a Costco-size irritation.
Are not valid, not applicable.

Here is the water, your body
the perfect temperature. Use as directed

or not: This is your time, your new everyday
flavour of possible. Tip your full face back

& drink it in. This uncareful Kool-Aid.
This wildberry-brilliant taste

of the way it should be.
Or could be.

Or is.

Kool-Aid
Jammers
Cherry

STORM
341 mls • 5% alc/vol

In Which Skinny-Dipping Temporarily Fixes a Life

There are days when life
reduces you to crackermeal,

to boxboard. There are
bleach burns & paper cuts.

Hurts, hazards, hot loss.
The consequential crush

of the everyday. Yes,
and there is this. This

slicing in face-first, this full-
contact festival, this water

on dry dusty skin. A cold wet everywhere
awakeness. First aid for the dry

damage of duty & compromise.
This coming back clean

to the compass of yourself.
After, a spot on a rock

& the taste of sun on everything.
Wet body brilliant as bottles.

In Which We Replace Garbage with Love

This place is famous for love, all brands
& standards. We who come here know love

is a verb, & we love with open hands.
On the road in, on the rock, in the falls,

we leave love wild, leave it wet & within
reach. We love without calculating or quitting

or letting up. We taste love, tumble in it, break it
open on the rock. We bleed from love

and come back with more. We light love on fire,
breathe it in, leave it like a small hot wish

when we go. But we will learn, or leave,
or get careful, so come look now:

We are fresh with love, & the days go by
like open windows.

SIGNATURE
du MAURIER

BLUE
STAR

A Few Words About the Idea of Litter

We know each other
by what we leave,

scattered trademarks
on all sides. From A&W

to Adidas, Kirkland to Keith's,
Blue Star to Black Horse

to Quidi Vidi Cream Ale.
But let's talk about the poisonous

math of it: Someone
somewhere is drinking oil

& vomiting money
in the gentle glow of the law

& it is not you or me & we cannot
end it at the outflow,

trying to bottle fumes. Not here,
not until we follow the money

back to the appliances of profit
itching in their overheated Oz,

gloved hands
on the throttle.

Gesture Goods

Praise the hands ripping open a package of cold Pop-Tarts.
Praise the palms on twist tops,

the Gatorade athletes hydrating on the move.
Praise the one-handed eating of cheeseburgers

& the vinegar tongues of the potato chip lovers.
Praise the tossing back, the open throat cooled

by a can of Palm Bay Strawberry Pineapple Vodka Spritz.
Praise the tasting, the eating, the slaking, the swallowed.

Praise the gestures, intimate & passing,
& wish they did not fall beside us

like shotgun casings, not
outlast us, not here or elsewhere

in some unseen away.

0 Trans Fat
0 gras trans
Miss Vickie's
SEA SALT &
VINEGAR
SEL MARIN ET
VINAIGRE DE MALT
1987
220 g

Mikveh: Blessing for Immersion in Living Waters

Praise what steeps open the slow seed
or washes away with wild currents

or wears through rock. Praise fresh & salt.
We come—holes in socks & our sincerely

bad hair—to your seas, springs,
daylighting streams. We stand

salt-skinned & on our last larynx, dry
as sponges before your many, your still,

your crash, your whole & wonderful wet.
Close again over our skin—*please!*

praise! help!—you life-waters you
fat fountains you cold tumble. Hold us

while we attend to transformations
wet & small. Rinse these secrets

in our hands like sweet pears.

Grease
Fighter
50%
Sunlight
Lemon Fresh
Citron frais

Mikveh: In Which We Submerge Three Times in the Middle Pool

Let's go to the water & get clean.
That slow cold current,

just before it all falls into the sea.
There. Let's tip forward

& go under. First time
for the body: that chill,

that simple sport of returning
to the skin. Again

for the mind. You who decided
to let yourself be curious—

let's bypass thinking,
quit the facts for a while,

risk our leading brand
sunlight, our pasteurized chances

of having it all.
To tip, to turn, to twist

open under water.
One more time for what is

wild in each of us,
the simple particles of being,

removed from the packaging
of thirst & hope.

After, you are clean as dishes.
Your skin sparkling cold.

Inside, what could be
a small window opening. No,

less than that. Light comes in
as if through a straw.

What is it?
This small *I'm sorry*

in one palm & *it was not you*
in the other.

Say it to yourself. Say it
to your face, your throat—

I'm sorry—say it where it hurts.
Say it for your gentle hands

when you did not know
to be a fighter. For all the things

you could not say. Or,
calculating costs, did not.

Allez go! Get it in your eyes,
in your hair, on your all-possible skin.

Know this, breathe it. If only
these wet seconds. Go under

& under & under,
break the seal

on the brilliant verb
of your body.

SOME DEFINITIONS

onset, *n.* I'm twenty and heading out, boats loaded, on a week-long ocean kayaking trip in Desolation Sound. Then, for no reason I understand, my arms are too heavy. Then we're turning back to shore. Then someone is carrying my boat. Then I'm in a bed up the road from the launch point for the rest of the week, crying, saying *don't touch my skin*. After seven days, we get back in the car and drive back to town. By the time we get home I feel like myself again. That's the first time.

exercise intolerance, *n.* It's hard to identify exercise intolerance with a 48-hour delay. At first, I can spend my Saturday kayaking down a river for seven hours, stopping only to eat a chocolate bar, and come home happy. Two days later, I might be playing frisbee when I collapse and spend days in bed crying. I can't make sense of my body. I keep trying to do the things I can do on the good days. The collapses come closer and closer together until there are no good days.

chronic illness, *n.* I'm taking six classes at university, commuting by bicycle, kayaking on weekends, working at the art store, planning trips. Then I'm in bed, struggling to make sentences. I'm mud-wrestling with lesbians in the back of the pickup truck for my first pride parade. Then I'm in my room for a week. I go out dancing. Then three days in bed. I garden. Bed. I'm dropping all my classes. I'm quitting one job, then another. It's a week. It's a month. It's six years.

insomnia, *n.* After a few months, I stop sleeping. I know it isn't medically possible, but the way I remember it, I don't sleep for six months. Or I don't sleep at night. I start falling asleep in classes. I can't bike up the hills on the way to school. Then I can't bike. Then I can't take the stairs. Then I cry while walking to the bus stop. At night in my bed, I lie awake and cry from tiredness. During one of my final exams, I see fog that isn't there start to fill the tiered lecture hall from the floor up.

diagnosis of exclusion, ***n.*** *You meet all the criteria for Chronic Fatigue Syndrome and there's no other explanation,* the doctor explains. A year of specialist visits. Fifty-two tests that have come back negative. It's not like knowing. *It will be useful on forms,* she says. It is useful on forms.

not knowing, ***n.*** I ask, *how do I live with not knowing?* I ask, *what is the most joyful way to live with not knowing*? I ask, *what did I love most about whitewater kayaking that wasn't whitewater kayaking?*

not knowing, ***v.*** I stop knowing what is strategic. I stop knowing what is a waste of time. I lie on a bed and stare at the ceiling. I sit on a cliff and stare at the ocean. I stop knowing that I'm straight. I stop knowing whether I'm willing to work for the government. I stop knowing I should have a career. I stop knowing what's next.

recovery, ***n.*** After six years, for no reason I understand, I start to get better. Slowly. Incompletely. I can work part-time. Then I can walk my boss's dog at lunch. Then I can go on a short hike with no hills. I think, briefly, there might be a beginning, middle, and end to this. I wonder what it will feel like to trust my body again.

trajectory, ***n.*** At twelve years, I join an outrigger paddling team but skip the races. I go on a summer road trip, sleep in a tent, take a one-hour surfing lesson. I enroll in grad school and work three part-time jobs and have anxiety attacks but not physical collapses. I bike across town to my co-op job and, once only, on a bet, bike the whole way up Burnaby Mountain instead of putting my bike on the bus. I ask a stranger to take a picture of me at the top of the road, one arm hoisting my bike into the air above my sweaty body. I decide that my dream of canoeing the Yukon River is perhaps no longer impossible. I sign up for a whitewater canoeing class.

concuss, ***v.*** A yellow canoe swung into the air over the instructor's head. Interrupted by my head. It's the second day of the whitewater canoeing class. I'm thirty-five. It begins again.

diagnosis, ***n.*** I am diagnosed with a mild traumatic brain injury. Then, when I'm still off work months later, they say post-concussion syndrome. Then someone suggests testing me for Lyme. I don't know what's Lyme disease and what's post-concussion but, nineteen years after I first get sick, there are words.

concussion, ***n.*** It comes back, the familiar fatigue, the brain fog, the exercise intolerance, the short-term memory loss. Except this time I can't read a book or use a computer. Or I can, but after ten minutes I collapse sobbing and shaking on the floor. This is my response to board games, Boggle, two people talking at the same time, the sound of cutlery and background conversation in a restaurant. This is my response to yoga, riding a bike, loud noises, trying to sort books by the call numbers on their spines. I write emails in five-minute shifts, looking away from the screen while I'm typing and then looking back to fix my mistakes. I struggle to remember words. It takes me a few months to return to work, several more months to make it to the end of a full workday. It takes a year before I can read a whole book, a middle grade novel with three-page chapters, to the end. It takes five years to start writing again. I don't go back to riding a bike or yoga or timed word games or watching 3D movies or ice skating or strenuous hikes or roller coasters or drag shows or festivals with amplified music or anything in a loud bar. Even now, sound still sometimes registers as pain. A fire alarm can bring me to my knees. Some days the sound of the HVAC in the ceiling is more than I can bear.

cure narrative, ***n.*** Sudden illness as the beginning, cure as the resolving climax, and everything between as a vast miserable middle to get through.

cure narrative, ***n.*** *Overcoming! Conquering! Body as battleground! Illness as underworld! Cure as redemption! Triumph-over-tragedy! Solved by science! Hero's journey back to health! Illness as lesson! Effort as morality! Epiphany as cure!* Solved, fixed, healed as the only possible character arc for sick and disabled protagonists. Inspiration or tragedy. Erasure.

not knowing, ***v.*** Should I be doing more to try to figure this out? Less? If I didn't focus so much on my health, would I enjoy my life more? Am I not sick anymore but only lazy? What will it take for me to eradicate *lazy* from my vocabulary? How much harm am I doing to others when I talk about myself this way? Who are my people? Am I allowed to use the word disability? What do I aim for when it's not recovery? Am I doing my best? Why do I think I have to be doing my best? Will my new doctor believe me? Which outfit says sick enough to deserve care but presentable enough to get it? Is it really Lyme? How much money have I spent trying to understand this? When will I shake this desire for a magical fix?

mikveh, ***n.*** I think I do my changing in the water.

Punch Bowl

All words (except titles) from garbage collected at Punch Bowl Pond near St. John's, NL.

Some Rules—

1. The cold water is a portal
   that can transport you
   only to wherever you
   already are.

2. It works or it doesn't,
   like all magic.

Portals

As a child they were a dim
peripheral, something

sideways. Appearing
to the eye only

as they were about
to close. A hum at the edge

of a formal garden
that called to us, sparked

hasty side-leaps into a hedge
or flowerbed. Later,

they daylighted as doors:
painted hardwood,

mosaic entryway. Inert until
cast to life with words:

on the other side a world in
which, that holds, where we—

something about speaking
or boldness. Maybe truth,

where truth is the future tense
of spells cast. The place beyond

re-made as spoken & looking,
as parallel universes often do,

otherwise much like this.
Now I dive towards the perfect

doorway of my outline,
the rippling of a beaded curtain

about to part. Now I surface, wet
with crossing.

A&W
NOTHING COMPLEMENTS
CREAMY
BURGERS
quite like creamy
ROOT BEER.
Burger Bliss

LIGH

We Break the Ice with a Garden Shovel for the First Swim of Spring

Cash & carry. In & out.
A refining fire that jacks

you up & tongues off
your pale undercoating

of salt. Cold shock-starts
your animal breath,

shakes you like a can.
Last season's slag & mildew

replaced by a buzz
below the skin:

carbonated, unruly,
ready for what comes.

Can We Talk about Pleasure?

About limb-splayed
leaps & wet hair flips,

faces that surface in cool
fog screaming *I AM ALIVE*

for all the highway to hear.
Our underwater skin

in slo-mo, corrugated
by water & speed. Yes

to pleasure, & yes again,
until we can splash

back into this at will, yes.
Off-season, anywhere,

easy as the salty snacks
we are now, floating open

& un-sorry. Oysters
sliding from our half-shells

into the tipped-back
face of creation.

GOURMET
D
Smoked Oysters
Huîtres Fumées
READY TO SERVE
PRÊT À SERVIR
PRODUCT OF CHINA • PRODUIT DE LA CHINE

Skinny-Dipping in the Rain

August's open hydrant
of heat starts to cool

at last. Air dampens,
water darkens

around you. Lie back
into it. Turn your wet face

up & feel it begin
soft as sugar

across your nose,
then build to pop-rock fizz.

You are 60% water, give or take.
Eyes closed, let your round edges

rise into the barbed sting of so many
small
          hard
                    candies,

this insistent three-way
of water & water

& you.
After, a still cup

overflowing.
Wet tiara of hair.

This wonderful warm, this perfect
outline that twists with you,

water to water. *O skin*
of my skin. O water.

O world.

POP ROCKS®
Strawberry
ARTIFICIALLY FLAVORED
POPPING CANDY
NET WT. 0.33 OZ (9.5G)
TASTE THE

MOON

Night Swimming, Fall Equinox

For Lisa

Remember
under that go-go moon

how we twisted
out of even our names?

Everything unbottled
& showing & tongued

by cold water? Brave
& algebraic, we added

our daily recommended
allowance of heat to the still

water, each of us with our
signature spark

split between one moon
& the other—

half island
& half hot star.

In Which It Takes a Long Time to Recover

You bottle your sparks in vinegar
& hold them close to your ribs

—glassed in, lightless.
You will learn from your power outage.

You will be different this time & no,
not as in smaller. One day

you want to carry this whole
tired humpty dumpty

to the smooth water & pour it out.
Want to ask, *how do I make this*

small star speak again.
Want to write your unpracticed face

in still water & find
how it ignites.

Original
85 g

In Which Skinny-Dipping Restores a Voice

You have come to speak one-on-one
with the world. Not danger exactly,

just that your fire has become harmless,
your hope tastes like aspartame

& your thirst cannot remember
what it wants. An illustrated book

of hazards & antibodies & small
careful passions. Your questions,

plastic tools that leave no mark.
What is it you want? The world

holds out its world-sized palm
filled with water. Leave your bright

packaging on the rock. Make cold contact.
Your face, your ribs. Your assembled

damage & cravings. Stay under.
Lose your left & your right. Lose your receipts

& your schedules & your adhesive
outline. Come back up breathless &

breathe. That harmless fire—
not yours. You are alive. Your fine fat

facts. Your unsweetened tongue.
Speak now like a child who is

also an alligator. Speak your hazards,
your hardwood, glass-fibred barbs

& kiln-dried wants. Library of starched
passions, impossible flames small

as almonds. Speak the apples
of your green-bodied attention

& your unauthorized animal moons.
Speak hot & necessary like calories,

like antibodies.
Like fire.

SOME DEFINITIONS

voice, *n.* How dare I use my voice for this small and personal purpose, this pocket of individual joy, when there are more pressing crises and injustices?

porousness, *adj.* Swimming in wild places makes me porous to the realities of the world. The somatic opposite of keeping my shields up on a crowded subway. I open to the subtle delights of rippling light reflected onto overhanging rock, the held note of a loon's call, water striders scooting across the surface and their bulbous shadows below. When I see garbage, I can look past my initial annoyance at individual behaviour and instead trace it back to the grievous harm done by the colonial and capitalist systems that the concept of 'litter' was designed to obscure. I am more open to everything around me—the wonders, and the violences also. In rushes joy. In rushes climate crisis. In rushes Gaza.

water colonialism, *n.* Boil water advisories in Indigenous communities across Canada. Mercury poisoning in Grassy Narrows. Methylmercury contamination in Muskrat Falls. The politician saying, *eat less fish*. The Ontario government allowing a transnational corporation to extract water on an expired permit while local communities face drought restrictions. The Israeli military bombing water infrastructure in Gaza, pumping salt water through tunnels and destroying the ground water. Soldiers shooting rainwater tanks in the West Bank, filling wells with cement. Meanwhile, swimming pools in illegal settlements.

voice, *n.* How, even after, or in the face of? While witnessing? When each year worse, more frequent, increasingly unpredictable? When, with impunity? In an ongoing? During an escalation of? How, when every day?

ecological grief, ***n.*** As I stop blaming my discomfort on people who visit these ponds and rivers and 'litter,' two things happen. I find myself surrounded by evidence of other people's joy, which is an unexpected delight. And as the 'litter panic' subsides, but the problem of single-use packaging remains visible, I become aware of a larger-scale ambient grief about extractive colonial relationships to land. I am left to navigate a more intimate relationship with climate grief and ecological destruction. With the impact of power structures that shape and make possible my everyday life. At times I am, quite literally, swimming in it.

Nothing Is Wrong, I Tell Myself

A studio apartment worth of words
where there used to be

a world—but I guess I'm lucky.
Lucky, to have hurt my brain

just a little. A little as in *I'm fine*,
mostly, except those things that turned

fishlike—sleep for example,
words. Words went slippery,

hard to hold in the mouth
that used to run

artesian, no, what's the word?
What's the word is how I find myself

here, at this pile of empty bottles
and candy wrappers, settling for recognition,

not creation. Not creation, certainly,
this searching labels for something

close enough to what bangs
on the mind's door. The mind's door,

which opens and shuts
like a haunted memory game,

flipping cards up one by one,
hoping to hit on whatever it was I wanted

to say. I wanted to say something
true and plain but my mind

crossed, boggled, left me
to jigsaw my way

towards—*is this even speaking?*
Even speaking as the *I* in *I Spy*

is hard these days: call it laziness,
call it form. Call it form, sure, these limits,

this room of too few words whose walls
I hit first, before my own faltering.

Before my own faltering I had no need
of this slapdash muckery,

insects crawling in the sugary spills
on the kitchen table where I sit

sorting garbage, trying to re-teach my brain
how to say what I mean

in brash borrowed imperative
and fact-proof superlative—

is there some badge to be had
taking words back

from their marketing day jobs
or am I just waiting for echolalia

to become self-aware? Self-aware:
to look in a mirror and say *it me!*

It me, as we say of grumpy cats
and tumbling pandas

and the incandescent rage of the sun
behind a small backlit figure,

swimming in a polka dot bikini
as if nothing is wrong.

Nothing is wrong, I tell myself
some mornings, walking the flooded lawn

back to the porch after an early swim
across the flooded lake.

And across the flooded lake, the exuberant
nasal haranguing of the geese,

it me, it me. It me, that original cry
in the face of the first mirror

when we climbed with new feet
out of whatever held us, wet

and indistinguishable. Indistinguishable as we
once were from each other and the world, no gap

between to be monetized and leveraged.
But monetized and leveraged,

swimming in terms and conditions,
how now do we look back at the flooding

lake, at the garbage pile, and let ourselves recognize
ourselves, let our small voices be filled—

a rising up, a song. A song: *it me.*
It me, grieving.

SOME DEFINITIONS

swim ***v.*** intransitive 1.a. To move along in or on water by movements of the limbs or other natural means of progression. ...2.d. Phrases in which *swim* is opposed to *sink*; esp. sink or swim (occasionally swim or drown), used spec. in reference to the ordeal of suspected witches, hence *figurative* = 'whatever may happen'. 3.a. To move or float along on the surface of the water, as a ship. Now *poetic*. 3.b. To be conveyed by a body floating on the water. Also *figurative* as in phr. 'to be in the same boat with'... 7.a. Of the head or brain: To be affected with dizziness; to have a giddy sensation. Also, of the head, to swim round = to be in a whirl. 7.b. Of the eyes: To be troubled or blurred: with mixture of sense 8. To abound *with* swimming animals. 9.a. To float, be immersed or steeped, *in* a fluid... 9.b. *figurative*. To be immersed or sunk *in* pleasure, grief, etc.... 10.b. *figurative*. To be full to overflowing *with*. —OED

nervous system regulation, ***n.*** In the water, my nerves finally stop multi-tasking. None of them are afraid. None of them are wondering what they look like in a bikini. There is no room for looking between my skin and the skin of the world. Each nerve registers the same smooth touch of the water. They are in agreement. There is no chatter, no emergency council. Slowly, my nerves open like barnacles, reaching their slight sightless fronds out into the living water.

swimming, ***n.*** The time I feel most uncomplicatedly at home in my queer, chronically ill body. Or, for a moment, at home in the world.

anhedonia, ***n.*** The inability to feel pleasure. I learn this word after my second concussion.

co-regulation, ***n.*** "From a polyvagal perspective, social interaction is all about facilitating co-regulation. That is: our body's ability to simultaneously project and receive signs of safety with others. And, in doing so, allow us to regulate our nervous system so as to experience the states conducive to health, growth, and restoration." —Stephen W. Porges and Seth Porges, *Our Polyvagal World*

swimming, ***n.*** As my only way, some days, of being held.

shiny, ***adj.*** Why are we attracted to shiny things? Scientists think it's an evolutionary adaptation that moves us to prioritize noticing anything that glints, glosses, shines, sparkles. Anything that reflects like water. We are constantly scanning for water. Our preference for glossy paper over matte increases when we're thirsty.

co-regulation, ***n.*** A process of relational nervous system regulation based on social connection and communication of safety cues with other people or mammals. So why does swimming alone seem to do the same for me? When I say solitude do I actually mean co-regulation with the more-than-human world? When I say wild swimming, do I mean in places where I can more easily receive safety cues from the land?

survival joy, ***n.*** Some days, after the second concussion, it takes every ounce of my available will to get into the car and drive myself to the pond. I cry on the walk in. I cry on the walk out. But the moment I dive in, I feel not simply pleasure, but physical joy. This reminds me that I am still capable of experiencing sensory pleasure, the joy of being in my skin, of touching my skin to the world. I call this 'survival joy.' This is me clawing my way back towards the possibility of feeling okay. And while I might not be able to hold onto it for long, just knowing it is possible keeps me going. Amid whatever monsters, I have a door in my brain marked: *Here be joy.*

swim, ***v.*** By movements of the limbs of suspected witches. Hence, whatever may happen to the water. To a body. To a brain. To be affected with sensation—a whirl, eyes blurred, swimming animals. Immersed. Steeped. Sunk. In pleasure, grief, etc. Overflowing *with.*

Big Punch Bowl

All words (except titles) from garbage collected at Big Punch Bowl Pond near St. John's, NL.

Twist This Lifted Lexicon

out from under licenses & trademarks.
Abandon the shareholders. *Bye-bye. F off*

sponsors, surveillance, all that *better, best, betcha.*
Choicest words—you little speak-weasels

bursting with buzz & beaucoup. Wanting to want,
for once, what is worth wanting.

Dial up the oysters on ice, the dark saltlick
of stars, your hot spite, your too much, your splash,

your more more more. Bring that whole inflatable
pharmacy of bafflement. Whose page?

Your page. Whose story?
Whose truthful smoking core?

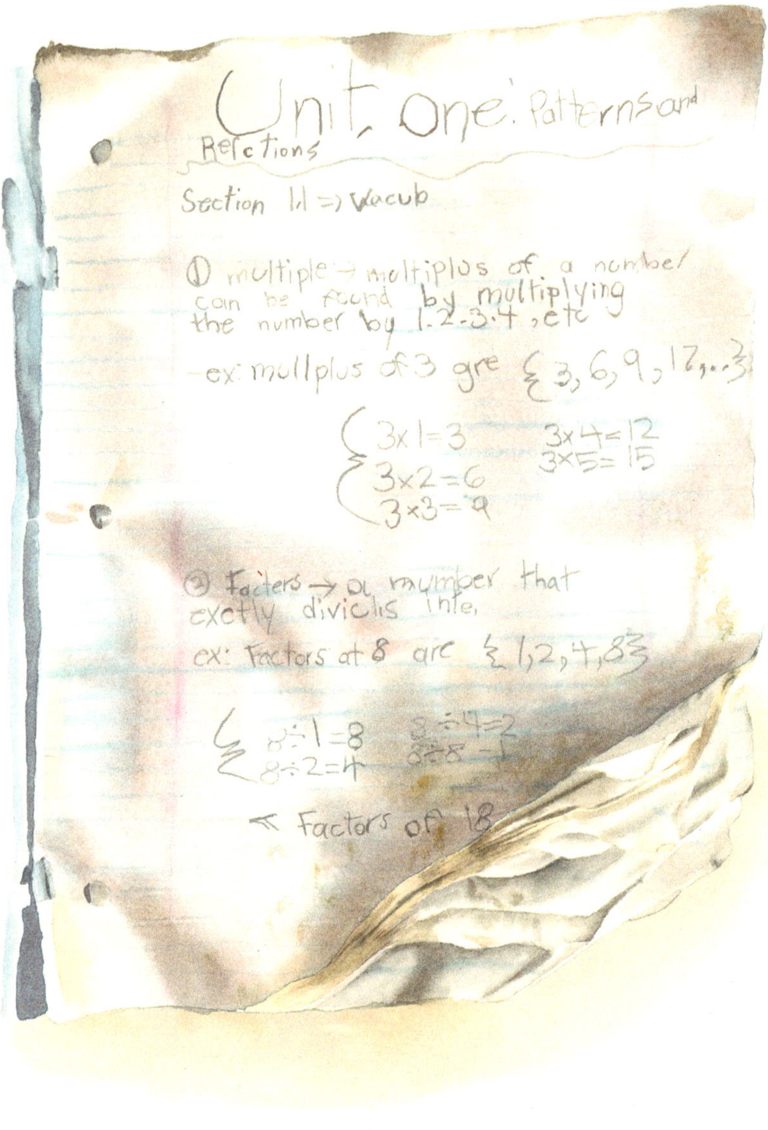

Unit one: Patterns and
Refctions
Section 1.1 => Vacub
① multiple → multiplos of a number
can be found by multiplying
the number by 1.2.3.4 , etc
-ex: mullplus of 3 are {3, 6, 9, 12, ...}
3x1=3
3x2=6
3x3=9
3x4=12
3x5=15
② Facters → a number that
exctly diviclis inle,
ex: Factors at 8 are {1,2,4,8}
8÷1=8
8÷2=4
8÷4=2
8÷8=1
Factors of 18

In Which It Is Hard to Talk About What Brings Us Here

How to talk about what we want
to undo in the cold water: one toe,

then the other. Look, it's like this.
Humpty Dumpty had a great—

Each day it costs more to talk
in code, to solve for *x*, to best some beast

& not speak of it. The hours build up
like creosote. A danger all smoke

& no flames is still danger. We hold it
together, paste over it, light it delightfully

like lunch for the internet. Or tea
in fine china. Once, we wanted

to crush all the king's saucers
& all the king's cups. Now we can't seem

to stop smiling through the smoke.
The world asks only that we try.

How much? says the woodchuck.
Woodchuck knows a lot about *on & on*.

About *could & would*
& *if*.

Body Image I

So much circus to
undo & not knowing,

in the meantime, how
to find the safe side

of caring.

zero
Glaceau
vitaminwater

adidas
SPORT ENERGY
3
BODY
HAIR
FACE
RECHARGING
ENERGISANT

I Take My Concussion for a Swim

Dear noggin, holding close your soft
sac of thoughts, thirsts, problems.

Bits of personality shaken,
re-assembled under pressure

& all the while, your grey vinyl
spinning, keeping me alive.

Still, some days it's discount karaoke—
words approximate, packing distance.

Patched, I bring you, prized & alive,
I bring you to the famous water.

All the tiredness, constant translation,
the holding up, holding on—into & under

the cold. When we surface,
we are tongueless

as grapefruit, edges steaming
with something not alphabet

or temperature. Distance
& translation both stilled

as a gentle beast
addresses the air.

Body Image II

The world shakes its
short shorts on the street.

Is it okay to have a crush
on myself, it asks?

The world is warning itself
not to & then reading

the comments. *Is it still okay,*
world wants to know,

to carry this fat like cash
& breathe?

Crush
Pineapple
Ananas

80 Pages
27.6 cm x 21.2 cm
Ruled 7 mm • Ligne 7 mm
EXERCISE BOOK
CAHIER D'EXERCI
NAME/NOM
SUBJECT/SUJET

Pond as Venn Diagram

as it is—

failing &

tired &

messy &

sore &

sick

& you
surface in
the middle,
meet the
middle with
your whole
elastic
animal—
alive &
not absent
from
anywhere

—as it could be

fluid

held

singing

sacred

& whole

Body Image III

Is it possible to step
into the water

as if into the entire ache
of the many-bodied world

that doesn't know,
in pieces,

if it is lovable?

JONES
CANE SUGAR SODA

100% ARABIC
fresh... Toujours frais...
fresh... Toujours frais

Writing the Same Poem Over & Over

This corrugated plot, bent in on itself,
each page ending *cool-bodied* or *electric*

or whatever word I can find for *briefly*
okay. Of course we've been there already.

This lifetime of choosing the thing,
learning the road by laying it exactly

where it was. Like potato chips or returning
to the breath: again, again. They say

the brain is plastic, only they use better words—
longer, less brittle. I wish I was longer & less

brittle, my attention for sitting with words,
I mean, my brain. If I cannot spell it out

in candy wrappers, the place I want
to belong, here is the driveway in, flattened

daily by returning. Here, the still water
I practice being held by, again,

again, until I carry it like a single apple
blossom, sheltered from the wind.

Somewhere in me could be a whole tree
of blossoms, opening their chances

& all I have to do is find the road
again.

Body Image IV

This underwater
outline is a selfie

drawn in sweet tea.
Is the shifting trace work

of a hand-held star.
Is the coughing up

of america &
other marketing.

The water
quotes your skin

back to your skin.
Attend to this

contact. The
tannin-dark pond,

these thighs,
the rippling

folds of light
mapping the way

for something like
love or repair.

THÉ GLACÉ

Maybe a Body

You want to speak plainly.
To unbutton, unzipper. To step

out of one pant hole
& then the other.

Your words without pockets
or pleats. But you hoped

it would sound different.
You are tired. You have been tired

for on & on & you're not sure
how to make it mean something.

You're jealous of people
who sound like who they are.

You want to sound like that
too. If you knew

what you weren't ready
to say, you'd say that.

You dive into the pond.
Someone lends you fruit inflatables

& you fall naked off pineapples
& large pitless peaches.

You float without a shell.
After, you sit still naked with friends,

not yet having solved
whatever you each don't like

about yourself. Everyone
on that ice-smoothed rock

believes everyone else is perfect,
just not them. Maybe you want

beauty, or to unleash
a new form. Maybe a body

doesn't need to be solved.
Maybe this is it, how the sun feels

everywhere, how you're
never surface-to-surface

so completely as in the water,
the pond up every nerve.

The way you talk to each other
after, skin still wet.

The warm wind. Thoughts
thawing into smaller

& smaller kernels,
from *worthy*

to *brave* to
here.

SOME DEFINITIONS

disposable, ***adj.*** "designed to be thrown away after one use." —OED

litter, ***n.*** A single word that encapsulates the strategy of blaming individual consumers for public waste problems in order to protect the right of companies to produce disposable packaging. A 1950s PR campaign so successful that the concept has crept into our lexicon as a synonym for waste, trash, discards, garbage—effortlessly injecting corporate-funded misdirection into our daily conversations.

disposability, ***n.*** A convenient solution to the stagnant sales in post-war America, when households already owned most of the consumer goods they needed, but companies needed to keep growing indefinitely to be profitable. From single-use packaging to planned obsolescence, disposability had to be invented and people had to be convinced to buy it. Industry marketing helped manufacture obsessions with hygiene, convenience, and aesthetic trends in their efforts to sell people items that they already owned.

away, ***adv.*** "[Disposability] assumes access to land. It assumes that household waste will be picked up and taken to landfills or recycling plants that allow plastic disposables to go 'away.' Without this infrastructure and access to land, Indigenous land, there is no disposability." —Max Liboiron, "How Plastic is a Function of Colonialism" *Teen Vogue*

plastics, ***n.*** "The future of plastics is in the trash can." —Lloyd Stouffer, 1956 National Plastics Conference

litterbug, ***n.*** A mutant sewer-dwelling character with a cockroach exoskeleton in Marvel comics. A cautionary 1961 Donald Duck short film about littering. The central crime in Arlo Guthrie's famous 1967 anti-war anthem, "Alice's Restaurant Massacree". Another name for the giant burrowing cockroach in Australia. A person who leaves garbage in public places.

litter, ***n.*** When I read these poems in public, people applaud and ask if it's an anti-littering campaign.

bottle laws, ***n.*** When the introduction of disposable bottles and cans led to a garbage crisis in public places and on agricultural land, and Vermont farmers complained that their cows were ingesting broken glass from bottles thrown into haystacks, the state responded by passing the U.S.'s first "bottle law" in 1953. This law banned throwaway bottles and required that drinks be sold in re-usable containers. Similar legislation was proposed in other states, threatening companies whose profit-margins and expanded distribution systems depended on single-use packaging.

Keep America Beautiful, ***n.*** A "litter prevention" non-profit created in 1953 by the American Can Company and Owens-Illinois Glass Company, inventors of the disposable can and bottle. Funded by industry giants like Coca-Cola, Pepsi, Philip Morris, and the Dixie Cup Company. A powerful and well-funded lobby organization that opposed regulation of single-use containers, and pushed for anti-litter legislation instead. The reason the bottle law was allowed to expire in Vermont, and no similar legislation was passed elsewhere. A masterclass in greenwashing before the word greenwashing existed. Keep America Beautiful continues to operate today, describing itself as one of the US's largest environmental non-profits.

litter, ***n.*** I read poems about chronic illness, nervous systems, cognitive injury, naked bodies, pain, depression, capitalism, queer sex. *Is it an anti-littering campaign,* asks the audience member, the interviewer, the reviewer for the local newspaper.

litterbug, ***n.*** A portmanteau of *litter* and *jitterbug*, used in a NYC transit system etiquette poster in 1947, and popularized by Keep America Beautiful. "Don't be a litterbug, 'cause every litter bit hurts," read the public-facing anti-litter ads from Keep America Beautiful in the 1950s, while the organization worked behind the scenes to get rid of requirements for reusable bottles. A word that villainizes and sometimes even criminalizes individual consumer behaviour. A word that can lead to jail time in some jurisdictions. A word that promised to take the focus off regulating industrial production, and delivered.

recycling, ***v.*** Another PR strategy designed to shift attention away from the ecological harm inherent in the production of single-use packaging and, once again, focus blame on the individual end-consumer. The now ubiquitous three-arrow recycling triangle was the result of a design contest sponsored by the Container Corporation of America, and timed to coincide with the first annual Earth Day festivities in 1970.

carbon footprint, ***n.*** Popularized as part of a British Petroleum public relations campaign to shift attention away from the large-scale ecological harm done by the oil industry and focus blame on individual consumer actions. British Petroleum launched the first "Carbon Footprint Calculator" as part of an ad campaign in 2004.

plastics, ***n.*** "The plastics industry is what's bailing out the oil industry right now." —Max Liboiron, *Media Indigena Podcast*

systemic, ***adj.*** How do we break the spells that keep colonial power and corporate profit invisible?

Roblin Lake

All words (except title) taken from garbage found at local beaches and lakes near Ameliasburgh, ON.

How Long Until No Longer This? Notes on Incomplete Research Into How Long It Will Take These Mylar Balloons in the Shape of a 5 and a 3 to Decompose Entirely

Longer than a punch?

Longer than a facepalm?

Longer than an on-ramp?

A toilet flush?

The B-side of a record?

53 bags of Cheetos?

Longer than a sonogram?

Than the glow of mini glow sticks?

Longer than a hookup?

Unrefrigerated yogurt?

The caffeine in 53 double doubles?

The pull of contained helium?

53 bacterial generations?

A power outage?

53 games of Super Mario?

53 sticks of gum?

Unaddressed thirst?

A honeymoon?

Longer than deli meat?

Summer camp?

A crush?

An egg carton?

The repair work on the expressway?

A waxed apple?

53 openings of a sunflower?

Longer than flushable wipes in the septic?

Longer than the presidency?

53 bars of soap?

The shelf life of hard candy?

Frozen assets?

High school?

Longer than the life celebrating 53?

Longer than the company that made the balloons?

Longer than a beer can?

Longer than a king?

Longer than copyright?

The diet industry?

The anti-litter league?

The dream of recycling?

The corporation that owns the company that made the balloons?

The oil lobby?

The first 53 flooded cities?

The wealth of the corporation passed down to the children?

The children of the children?

The glaciers?

The expressways?

Property rights?

Longer than the idea of away?

Longer than England?

Than borders?

Than commerce?

Longer than the damage?

Longer than the need?

Longer than clouds?

SOME DEFINITIONS

cold water swimming, *n.* A runner's high without the running. Exercise endorphins for a chronically ill body without risk of overexertion. The closest I have come to the full-throated endorphin rush I felt in my teens as a competitive paddler when I reveled in pushing my body to its limits. A way for me to thrill again, if sometimes only briefly, at being a person with a body.

cold water, *n.* Usually anything under 15°C. Or the temperature below which the physiological reactions of cold shock response and mammalian dive reflex kick in.

cold shock response, *n.* An autonomic nervous system response based on sudden immersion in cold water. Activation of sympathetic ("fight, flight or freeze") nervous system. Involuntary gasping, increased heart rate, hyperventilation, skin cooling, constriction of blood vessels at extremities.

mammalian dive reflex, *n.* An evolutionary adaptation in all mammals that maximizes potential dive time and minimizes the usage of oxygen. Triggered by breath-holding combined with cold water at the entrance of the nostrils. Activation of parasympathetic (the "safe and social" or "rest and digest") nervous system. Slowed heart rate, increased ability and reflex to hold the breath, constriction of blood vessels near extremities to prioritize blood flow to organs. Why people splash their faces with cold water to calm down.

cold shock response, *n.* Force yourself to breathe slowly and deeply. You'll get past it in ninety seconds or so.

mammalian dive reflex, *n.* This is the one that feels good. It should kick in after the gasping is over. Once I feel calm, I hold my breath and place my face against the water.

autonomic conflict, ***n.*** When the two branches of the autonomic nervous system send conflicting signals to the heart—*speed up! slow down!*—it can lead to dangerous arrhythmias or cardiac arrest. A good reason not to jump or dive into extremely cold water. Is it possible to be gentle while entering a frozen pond? I try.

cold water swimming, ***n.*** Not a remedy, not a biohack or productivity strategy, but a letting go of fixes and cures. Not weightlessness, but gravity in all directions, these hundred thousand feet of cold anchoring me to the world.

Cape Broyle

All words (except titles) from garbage collected at a swimming hole in Cape Broyle, NL.

Cold Shock Response

Gasp. Cautionless
mouthfuls. No skill or aim,

only appetite in gloves of slush.
Gasp, we grab at the air

before asking, *is there air?*
Alight with cold, classroom

potassium dropped in water.
Blood, punching. Our old code

calling. We gasp, cold bells
that cannot stop ringing.

Smartfood
POPCORN MAÏS SOUFFLÉ
WHITE CHEDDAR BLANC
200 g

Mammalian Dive Reflex

We understand the cold
by putting our faces

into it. The water is not
symbolic, not an exam

question, not proof.
Blood stalls in our limbs

& at our limits. The good
pump slows its trade,

keeps the light on only
in the necessary kernel.

When we surface, a glazing
of cool sun, the quiet crush

of animal calm. Stand still,
I am testing your name.

We are mammals,
handsprings, children

with maps. Corn popping
in the soft air.

Blessing for the Swim Selfie

Layer by layer, let us onion
open into the sun. Let us swing,

pantsless as tolling bells,
into the green-gold water.

We are spilling from sugar
cones. We are mouthfuls.

We are sick & whole. Mages,
building boats of popsicle sticks

& emotions. Our hands are constellations
of Dorito dust, diving. We are

mathematics. Please, we are facts,
with faces & cameras as proof.

KitKat

After We Undress Quietly in the Sun

We are a queer candy
in the underwater light.

The sugar sting of the crush.
The ionic thirst & against

all odds, the quencher.
Like the lesbionic hand of god

rang a bell, like time spilled
green again in our laps

& we turned to one another,
soft as we dared.

SOME DEFINITIONS

swimming, ***n.*** The smallest possible distance between my body and a body of water.

Cold Swimming with Larches, Cape Broyle, Late October

I pause, knee-deep, thinking, *maybe*
the fuck not. Then, then—I'm in. I hold

my body against the fire of those ninety seconds,
that first gasping panic. Force myself to exhale

through tight lips, to keep breathing
past the urge to exit. I push off, kicking hard

upstream, moving across the fast flow, eddy
to eddy until—*whoooooosh*—I let the current

take me. Then again. I step out into the afternoon,
skin red with cold, steaming. Eyesight sharpened,

colours saturated. I have ten minutes to get
dressed before I shiver uncontrollably, but my limbs

are loose now, languid, burning with a brief
and radiant heat. I have to remind myself

to get my pants on, to hurry, to drink
the scalding tea. But everything shines

and all I want is to take pictures:
the sun on the river, the backlit leaves.

Even as I pull back onto the highway,
the larches flare yellow, in sharp focus

against the evergreen blur as I speed back
to get warm. We have our altars to the disappearing

sun. Our SAD lamps, our vitamin D,
our SSRIs and morning walks and tinctures

as we tip away from our nearest, most
irreplaceable star. Whatever on this earth

holds the sun. The river-worn
bedrock still warm into evening.

Fat berries after frost. A face turned,
holding the late-day light every second

as it goes, holding, holding.
We seal up rosehip jelly

or peach halves in shining jars, fold
our small moments over and over,

coil them tight into words, into
fewer words, language

photovoltaic
under pressure,

a battery, a box
for a small spring

-loaded joy, complete
with the angle of the light

the speed of the car,
the impossible

way I see each
larch needle

individually electric
with sun and dying,

eyes skimming branches,
bundles of fine shining needles,

my mind like a thumb over a fine-toothed comb,
each muted ping, ping, the larches squealing yellow,

a quickening under the skin, a whetting, a painful
re-awakening to cold and colour and—

Will I look back and say, *that*
was the year the larches saved my life?

Is it the medication that allowed me
to see the larches? Or the cold water

that allowed the endorphins that allowed
the angle of the afternoon light, or the larches,

the larches, holding the sun,
the larches, hot yellow with it,

as I hurtle past, the larches like hands
through which something is slipping

brightly.

SOME DEFINITIONS

litter, ***n.*** 1a. A bed. *Obsolete...* 2a. A vehicle in use down to recent times, containing a couch shut in by curtains, and carried on men's shoulders or by beasts of burden. 2b. A framework supporting a bed or couch for the transport of the sick and wounded. 3. Straw, rushes, or the like, serving as bedding... 4. Odds and ends, fragments and leavings lying about, rubbish; a state of confusion or untidiness; a disorderly accumulation of things lying about. —*OED*

litter, ***n.*** I lie about in disorder. I swim in it. I am odds and ends. Fragments, leavings. I am confusion and untidiness. I contain couches. I am a queer accumulation. I am sick and I am wounded and I am carried.

Beachy Cove

All words (except titles) from garbage collected at Beachy Cove, NL.

Your Discarded Grocery Receipt as an Archeology of Joy

I see a hot car full of femmes & snacks—
tortilla chips, strawberries, smoked chddr,

rstd nuts, dairy mlk mint. A fire, maybe.
Calm water cooling in the last of the light.

How many more watermelon weekdays?
These btrswt, unrefrigerated, blkberry-fat

days. You hold them like so many
wild eggs, like an old love lodged in your throat.

You silver the water like trout.
After, you toss president's choice cinnamon

into the fire. Reach up & catch that last
crmy english toffee in one hand.

WESTERN
NEWFOUNDLAND
BREWING CO
WILD COVE
OLD WORLD PUB ALE
BREWED IN PASADENA NL
946ML

MAPLE
LEAF
Vienna
Sausage

Every So Often You Love Your Body

You are
a queer village

undressing,
lifting your ________ ,

saying here,
here

is my ________ ,
embers alive.

Your thirst lowers
its open ________

to the water
& drinks.

Bonfire

We are sweaty & mustard
stained. Throats, apple

hard. End of day, dimly lit
beach. All roads, etc.

God pulls us aside,
one by one, says,

you are a catch.
Some run fully-clothed

into the water.
Some palm each other

like trout in the dying light.
We bank the fire

& sing slower. We lift
& keep each other.

We hold on:
this small

walnut
of joy.

French's
YELLOW

Song of Early May Ocean Swimming

Sing the wind-stung
strawberries

of our undressing.
Labels sliding, as if

from jars. Sing the athletic
mouth of the ocean.

One after the other
we run at it: Hello!

Hello! Hello, here
we are, our cold loud

lungs of gladness.

pop tarts
Frosted
Strawberry
fraises
400 g
8
pop tarts

SPORT
BEANS
PORTABLE POWER

April and I Take the Underwater Camera Swimming On the Last Weekend of Summer

In this dim underworld,
liquid embers free-form

on our frames, dressing us
as if we could, this easily,

be loved. Fibres of afterlight—
are we recording?—taste us

like snacks. I am delicious,
we are delicious. Bare

confectionary. We breathe
& our air is uncanny,

mirrored beans that pull, swell,
silver the water around us.

Here, in the messy bed
of these light lines, in this far-

flung signature of the sun,
we unwind on record,

slower, slower—*are you
getting this?*—like a change

coming due.

SOME DEFINITIONS

spell, ***v.*** Poetry as incantation, as speech act, as linguistic battery, as asynchronous co-regulation, as jam jars put up for the long winter. As technology for storing and transmitting—body to body, nervous system to nervous system—a state of being, a felt-sense of embodiment. What would I call this if I did not believe in magic?

swimming, ***n.*** The dream that my body could feel like this, my brain work like this. Even on land. And for a few hours, it does.

mikveh, ***n.*** Our first Friday at Witchcamp, just before sundown, a small handful of us gather on the side dock to learn and practice mikveh together. We each dip naked under the water three times. We watch each other to make sure nothing, not a hair, is left above water. We sing, we say to each other, *not a hair, not a hair.*

magic, ***n.*** Let this book be a spell for our survival joys. For joy in the midst of. For experiencing our bodies as whole. As failing and sacred, or sick and singing, or hurting and held. For care of our edges, for warding against harm. For holding water as sacred, for protection of all beings, for collective liberation. For whatever we need to be porous with the world and, even briefly, in love with it.

nigun, ***n.*** Still shoulder-deep in the lake, we face the fading sky and learn a nigun, a wordless Jewish tune. *La la lai lai lai lai.* The last note of the melody ascends, ends suspended, has no resolution except to return to the beginning.

Acknowledgements

These are the names I know for the places I swam while writing this book, the bodies of water that held my body, co-regulated with my nervous system, and helped my brain heal so that I could re-learn to write poetry after a head injury and through continuing chronic illness: Aquaforte River, Atlantic Ocean, Barren Pond, Beachy Cove, Big Otter Pond, Big Pond, Big Punch Bowl, Big River, Big Tunnel, Blast Hole Pond, Broad Cove Beach, Broad Cove Brook, Broad Cove Pond, Colliers Pool, Colliers River, Conception Harbour Overfalls, Cook's Brook, Credit River, Cupid's Pond, Dancing Place Pond, Duck Pond (Shea Heights), Duck Pond (Bauline), Eastport Beach, Echo Pond, Elora Quarry, Eramosa River, Fermeuse Harbour, Flatrocks/Middle Place/Longshanks (Cape Broyle), Freshwater Bay Pond, George's Pond, Goat Cove, Gooseberry Cove, Grand River, Guelph Lake, Gull Island Falls, Healey's Pond, Herring Neck Pond, Hopkins Bay, Hughs Pond, Jericho Beach, Jones' Cove, Kingman's Cove, Kitsilano Beach, Koshlong Lake (Halls Island), La Manche Ponds, La Manche River, La Manche Waterfall, Lake Eerie, Lake Huron, Lake Ontario, Locarno Beach, Long Point Brook, Lumsden Beach, Madden Falls, Manuel's River, Middle Brook Falls, Middle Pond, Moon Pond, Mudder's Gulch, Muskoka River, Neary's Pond, Northern Bay Sands, Northside Beach, Pacific Ocean, Piper's Hole River Estuary, Piper's Hole River, Punch Bowl, Roblin Lake, Rockwood, Salish Sea, Salmon Cove, Salmon Pool, Sandy Cove Beach, Sandy Cove Pond, Second Pond, Shade's Mills, Shallow Bay, Skerwink Trail Pond, Soldier's Pond/Beaver Pond, Soldier's Pond/Big Dam, Southern Pond, Southern River (Cape Broyle), St. Lawrence River, Teacup, The Brook, The Canyon, The Dam (Harbour Grace), The Falls (Bay Bulls), The Gates, The Tide (Harbour Main), The Trestle, Three Pond Barrens, Thunder Brook/ Leech Brook Falls, Topsail Beach, Topsail Bight, Tors Cove Pond, Waseosa Lake, Western Bay Overfalls, Western Cove Brook, White Cove Beach.

These waters and shores are part of the unceded ancestral territories and treaty lands of the Mi'kma'ki, Beothuk, Musqueam, Squamish, Tsleil-Waututh, Michi Saagiig/Mississauga, Attiwonderonk, Haudenosaunee, Anishinaabeg, and Wendat, and the Mississaugas of the Credit First Nation. Most of the book was written on the island of Ktaqmkuk (Newfoundland), the unceded traditional territory of the Beothuk and the Mi'kmaq.

As I scroll through photos and maps to remind myself of these (mostly colonial) place names, it feels impossible to talk about the places I love without acknowledging the colonial power structures through which I have come to live in these places. Witnessing the recent escalation of land theft, ethnic cleansing, and genocide in Palestine has pushed me to understand, in a more visceral way, how these same strategies of settler-colonialism—dehumanization, displacement, killing, weaponized starvation and illness, targeting of children and education, destruction of land-based sustenance and knowledge—were and are part of the continuing colonial violence on Turtle Island.

As a friend of mine says to her young child, when asked to explain things that seems unfair and unjust: *But it did not have to happen this way. But it does not have to stay this way. But many people are fighting to change this and we can too.* Another world—not based on empire, colonization, extraction, supremacy, and profit—I have to believe this, is possible.

~

This project, including both writing and illustrations, has been funded by generous grants from the Canada Council for the Arts, ArtsNL (including a grant to commission the illustrations), and the City of St. John's, plus writing residencies through the Al Purdy A-frame Association, the Halls Island Artist Residency, and Piper's Frith.

Many of the poems first appeared in the following journals and publications: *Canthius, Voices from the FOLD, Tinderbox Journal, Arc Poetry Magazine, Bracken Magazine, Juniper, Riddle Fence, The Fiddlehead, In Fine Form: A Contemporary Look at Canadian Form Poetry, Watch Your Head: Writers and Artists Respond to the Climate Crisis, The Goose: A Journal for Arts, Environment and Culture in Canada,* and *Grain Magazine.*

"I am Writing a Spell for your Nervous System" appeared online after winning the SPARKS Literary Festival Award. A suite of five poems titled "The Garbage Poems" was shortlisted for the 2015 CBC Poetry Prize and was published on CBC Books. "In Which Skinny-Dipping Restores a Voice" was exhibited as part of winning an NL Arts and Letters Award. Interviews and writing about the project have appeared in the *Newfoundland Quarterly, The Fiddlehead,* and *Future Possible: An Art History of Newfoundland and Labrador.*

Several passages in "Some Definitions" were adapted from my essay, "In Which Skinny Dipping Temporarily Fixes a Life," published in 2021 in *Impact: Women Writing After Concussion* (edited by E.D. Morin and Jane Cawthorne).

My gratitude to all of the editors and staff who keep these important publications and events alive and thriving.

~

Poems in the sections with place-based headings are made from words transcribed from the garbage found at that specific location, collected over the course of eight years. There are also three non-garbage poems (poems not built out of found text) interspersed between these sections: "I am Writing a Spell for Your Nervous System" "Cold Swimming with Larches, Cape Broyle, Late October," and "Nothing is Wrong, I Tell Myself."

Definitions credited to the OED are from the digital version of the *Oxford English Dictionary* (with thanks to the Vancouver Public Library for keeping this resource available), and are generally excerpted and/or simplified in format.

Definitions without sources are in my own words, but often draw from research sources. I am indebted to the books and articles below for helping to expand my understanding of some of my current obsessions, which include cold water swimming, nervous systems, and the politics, economics, history, and colonial power structures of consumer waste. I read widely while writing this book, but the sources noted below are those I found most useful for the topics in the "Some Definitions" sections.

Pages 55–56: Concepts of nervous system regulation and co-regulation are discussed in the context of polyvagal theory and somatic therapy, including the work of Stephen Porges, Deb Dana, Peter A. Levine, and others, with thanks to Marika Heinrichs for her help. The research connecting the appeal of shiny things to water (p. 50) includes "Taking a Shine to It: How the Preference for Glossy Stems from an Innate Need for Water" (2014) by Meert, Pandelaere, and Patrick.

Pages 79–81: Entries about the social and economic history of consumer waste, including bottle laws, disposability, plastics, Keep America Beautiful, and colonialism draw mostly on the work of Susan Strassner, Heather Rogers, and Max Liboiron. For a deceptively simple introduction to the relationship between plastics, disposability, and colonial access to land, read Liboiron's article in *Teen Vogue* called "How Plastic Is a Function of Colonialism (2017)." For a deeper dive, check out their book *Pollution is Colonialism* (2021), or any of their related work.
For in-depth social and economic histories of garbage, read Susan Strassner's *Waste and Want: A Social History of Trash* (1999), or Heather Rogers's *Gone Tomorrow: The Hidden Life of Garbage* (2005). For a critical history

of recycling and carbon footprint calculators, check out Samantha MacBride's *Recycling Reconsidered: The Present Failure and Future Promise of Environmental Action in the United States* (2011), and Mark Kaufman's "The Carbon Footprint Sham" (2020). For an overview of the history of Keep America Beautiful, see Bradford Plumer's "The Origins of Anti-Litter Campaigns" (2006), and Rudy Sanchez's "Keep America Beautiful Ran A Master Class In Corporate Greenwashing" (2021). For a wide-ranging archive of ideas, writing, research, primary sources, and other resources related to waste and pollution, see the *Discard Studies* website (discardstudies.com).

Pages 89–90: I've read too much to list on the topic of cold water swimming but for a good overview of the physiological science and a meta-analysis of scientific studies, see Tipton et al.'s "Cold water immersion: kill or cure?" (2017).

~

Writing is often a solitary act for me, but creating a book is not. This book is a reflection of the generosity, encouragement, support, community, dedication, and love that has surrounded the process of creating it. These past two years have been a particularly difficult time in my life, but the work of making this book has been a thread of unexpected joy running through all of it. Thank you, in particular:

to April White for the partnership that has gone far beyond the illustrations in this book, where an art crush became collaboration became friendship—working and swimming together has been one of the great joys of this book,

to Alayna Munce for gently pushing this manuscript beyond anything I had imagined for it, for encouraging me to try new forms, for promising that we'd swim while editing this book and making it happen (I cannot imagine a more joyful way to edit)—working with you as an editor has been a gift that I do not take for granted, to the Editorial Collective and everyone else at Brick Books for saying *yes,* for agreeing to publish the book in colour (despite logical reasons not to), and for continuing to be one of my favourite publishers in the world, to Alayna Munce for your vision as a publisher, not just for this book but for Brick Books as a whole, to Manahil Bandukwala for your careful attention to this manuscript through copy editing and production, for saving me from myself many times over, and for celebrating in a cold lake, to Brenda Leifso, Ashley-Elizabeth Best, and Britt Landry for figuring out how to make this book possible, and how to get it out into the world—it has been an honour to work with every one of you and I cannot imagine a better home for this project,

to Natalie Olsen for the stunning cover design, and for taking such care with the design of the entire book,

to Lisa Baird, dearest friend and first reader for most of what I write, for the kind of sustaining friendship I am so lucky to have found in this life,

to Don McKay who was the first person to say that the original five garbage poems should be their own book, who helped edit early drafts of this work, and who has so generously offered support and mentorship over many years,

to Amber Dawn, Michael V. Smith, and Eva Crocker for their beautiful words in support of this project, where blurbs are only the visible portion of a larger generosity,

to my feygele-shraybers writing group, and to my little poetry group in St. John's,

to everyone who read and provided feedback on these poems: Tia McLennan, Matthew Hollett, Maggie Burton, Lisa Richter, Zoey Peterson, Leah Horlick, Karen Solie, Kevin Connolly, Fatima Amarshi, Suvendrini Lena, Torri Blue, Amanda Proctor, Em Dial, Aline-Mwezi Niyonsenga, Alexandra McKay, Claire Bailey, Desiree Mckenzie, Joseph Donato, Veronique Synnott, Calypso André, to writing friends whose support has sustained me and my writing in other ways during this time: Carmella Gray-Cosgrove, Mado Christie, Susie Taylor, Alex Cafarelli, Bassam, Chris Lafazanos, Randy Drover,

to Matthew Hollett for creating the interactive website for this project where readers can hover over each word in the featured poems and see an image of the specific piece of source garbage, or try writing their own garbage poems: garbagepoems.com,

to my teachers, mentors, and classmates at the University of Guelph MFA program, with a particular nod to Kyo Maclear's Hybrid Forms class, which I took right before editing this book and which gave me tools and courage to step out past my usual habits of form,

to Sophia for introducing me to mikveh at Loon Lake in the 1990s and for teaching me the nigun I still sing to this day,

to my parents, Susan and John Swanson, who have always nurtured, celebrated, and shared my love of poetry,

to every body of water I swam in, and the people who swam with me, for sharing the joys and griefs of the eleven years in which this book came to be.

Anna Swanson is a queer writer and librarian. Her first book of poetry, *The Nights Also* (Tightrope Books, 2010), won the Gerald Lampert Memorial Award and a Lambda Literary Award. Her writing has been widely published in journals and appears in anthologies including *Best Canadian Poetry, Impact: Women Writing After Concussion, In Fine Form: The Canadian Book of Form Poetry, Watch Your Head: Writers and Artists Respond to the Climate Crisis*, and *Torah: A Women's Commentary*. She recently completed an MFA at the University of Guelph and lives in St. John's (on the island of Ktaqmkuk/Newfoundland) where she works as a poetry editor for *Riddle Fence Magazine*. Her special interests include collective liberation and wild swimming in all seasons.

April White makes art for tired people who struggle to exist in neoliberal capitalist society. April typically works with print media, watercolour, drawing, textiles, and performance. They hold a BFA from Grenfell Campus, Memorial University of Newfoundland and Labrador (2012) and an MFA from Concordia University, Montreal (2023). April is an award-winning artist whose work has exhibited extensively in the east coast of Canada. April loves tacos, cats, and wild swimming.

Library and Archives Canada Cataloguing in Publication
Title: The garbage poems / Anna Swanson ; illustrations by April White.
Names: Swanson, Anna, 1974- author |
White, April (April Mary Lynn), illustrator.
Identifiers: Canadiana (print) 20250212994
Canadiana (ebook) 20250213095
ISBN 9781771316613 (softcover)
ISBN 9781771316637 (PDF)
ISBN 9781771316620 (EPUB)
Subjects: LCGFT: Found poetry.
Classification: LCC PS8637.W365 G37 2025 | DDC C811/.6—dc23

We gratefully acknowledge the Canada Council for the Arts, the Government of Canada through the Canada Book Fund, the Ontario Arts Council, and the Government of Ontario for their support of our publishing program.

ONTARIO ARTS COUNCIL
CONSEIL DES ARTS DE L'ONTARIO
an Ontario government agency
un organisme du gouvernement de l'Ontario

Ontario

Canada

Canada Council for the Arts
Conseil des Arts du Canada

Edited by Alayna Munce.
Author photo by April White.
Illustrator photo by Anna Swanson.
The book is set in Practical Serif and Obviously Sans.
Illustrations by April White.
Design by Natalie Olsen.

BRICK BOOKS
487 King St. W.
Kingston, Ontario
K7L 2X7
www.brickbooks.ca

Though much of the work of Brick Books takes place on the ancestral lands of the Anishinaabeg, Haudenosaunee, Huron-Wendat, and Mississaugas of the Credit peoples, our editors, authors, and readers from many backgrounds are situated from coast to coast to coast in Canada on the traditional and unceded territories of over six hundred nations who have cared for Turtle Island from time immemorial. While living and working on these lands, we are committed to hearing and returning the rightful imaginative space to the poetries, songs, and stories that have been untold, under-told, wrongly told, and suppressed through colonization.